I0649092

Charles Johnson Maynard, C. J. (Charles Johnson) Maynard

A Catalogue of the Birds of the West Indies

Charles Johnson Maynard, C. J. (Charles Johnson) Maynard

A Catalogue of the Birds of the West Indies

ISBN/EAN: 9783744662031

Printed in Europe, USA, Canada, Australia, Japan

Cover: Foto ©Andreas Hilbeck / pixelio.de

More available books at **www.hansebooks.com**

A

CATALOGUE

OF THE

BIRDS

OF THE

WEST INDIES

WHICH DO NOT OCCUR ELSEWHERE IN NORTH AMERICA
NORTH OF MEXICO

BY

C. J. MAYNARD

———

NEWTONVILLE
C. J. MAYNARD
1898

INTRODUCTION.

The following is a catalogue of the Birds of the West Indies, exclusive of those found on the Islands of Trinidad and Tobago, which have not been recorded as occurring elsewhere in North America, north of Mexico.

While I have been greatly aided in making this catalogue by Mr. Charles B. Cory's excellent works upon West Indian Birds, it will be seen that I have been able to make a few changes in habitat of some of the species through my own observations, and have also added some new forms, all from the Bahamas. Descriptions of these, as well as notes upon some of the changes in habitat, nomenclature etc., may be found in No. 3, Vol. III, of my Contributions to Science which was issued a short time before the publication of this catalogue.

C. J. M.

DEDICATED
TO MY FRIEND
MARLAND L. PRATT
WHOSE ENTHUSIASTIC LOVE OF THE STUDY OF
OOLOGY HAS BEEN THE ORIGIN
OF THIS BOOK.

CHECK-LIST.

1 **AESTRELATA JAMAICENSIS** (Bancr.).
   Blue Mountain Petrel.
   Jamaica.

2 **SULA CORYI** Mayn.
   Cory's Gannet.
   Little Cayman.

3 **DAFILA BAHAMENSIS** (Linn.).
   Bahama Duck.
   Bahamas; Antilles.

4 **DENDROCYGNA VIDUATA** (Linn.).
   Bahama Tree Duck.
   Bahamas and Antilles.

5 **DENDROCYGNA ARBOREA** (Linn.).
   Cuban Tree Duck.
   Cuba.

6 **ARDEA BRUNNESCENS** Lemb.
   Cuban Green Heron.
   Cuba.

7 **ARDEA BAHAMENSIS** Brewster.
   Bahama Green Heron.
   Bahamas.

8 **RALLUS MACULATUS** Bodd.
   Spotted Rail.
   Cuba.

9 RALLUS CORYI   Mayn.
    Cory's Rail.
    Andros, New Providence, Rose Island, Highburn
Key, Bahamas and Jamaica.

10 PORZANA CONCOLOR   (Gosse.).
    Jamaica Rail.
    Jamaica.

11 PORZANA FLAVIVENTRIS   (Bodd.).
    Yellow Vented Rail.
    Cuba; Jamaica.

12 FULICA CARIBAEA   (Ridgway.).
    Carribean Coot.
    Guadeloupe and St. John.

13 OEDICNEMUS DOMINICENSIS, Cory.
    San Domingo Land Plover.
    San Domingo.

14 EUPSYCHORTYX SONNINII   (Temm.).
    White-faced Partridge.
    St. Thomas.

15 COLINUS BAHAMENSIS Mayn.
    Bahama Bob-white.
    New Providence, Bahamas.

16 COLINUS CUBANENSIS   (Gould.).
    Cuban Bob-white.
    Cuba.

17. NUMIDA MELEAGRIS   Linn.
    Guinea Fowl.
    Cuba, San Domingo, Jamaica. Porto Rico, and
Barbula.

18 COLUMBA CORENSIS Gmel.
    Purple-throated Pigeon.
    Antilles.

19 COLUMBA CARIBAEA Linn.
    Carribean Pigeon.
    Jamaica and Porto Rico.

20 COLUMBA INORNATA Vig.
    Slaty Pigeon.
    Greater Antilles.

21 **ENGYPTILA JAMAICENSIS** (Linn.)
  Jamaica Dove.
  Jamaica.

22 **ENGYPTILA COLLARIS** Cory.
  Cayman Dove.
  Grand Cayman.

23 **ENGYPTILA WELLSI** Lawr.
  Wells's Dove.
  Grenada.

24 **ZENAIDA SPADICEA** Cory.
  Grand Cayman Dove.
  Grand Cayman.

25 **ZENAIDA RUBRIPES** Lawr.
  Grenada Ground Dove.
  Grenada.

26 **ZENAIDA RICHARDSONI** Cory.
  Richardson's Dove.
  Little Cayman and Cayman Brac.

27 **COLUMBIGALLINA BAHAMENSIS** Mayn.
  Bahama Ground Dove.
  Bahamas.

28 **COLUMBIGALLINA INSULARIS** Ridgw.
  Cayman Ground Dove.
  Grand Cayman.

29 **COLUMBIGALLINA JAMAICENSIS** Mayn.
  Jamaica Ground Dove.
  Jamaica.

30 **GEOTRYGON CRISTATA** (Temm.)
  Purple-collared Quail Dove.
  Jamaica.

31 **GEOTRYGON MYSTACEA** (Temm.)
  Green-headed Quail Dove.
  Guadeloupe, Santa Lucia and Grand Terre.

32 **GEOTRYGON CANICEPS** Gundl.
  Cuban Quail Dove.
 Cuba.

33 REGERHINUS WILSONII (Cass.)
    Wilson's Hawk.
    Cuba.

34 REGERHINUS UNCINATUS (Temm.)
    Blue Hawk.
    Grenada and Antilles.

35 FALCO CARIBBAEARUM Gmel.
    Carribean Sparrow Hawk.
    Lesser Antilles.

36 FALCO DOMINICENSIS Gmel.
    San Domingo Sparrow Hawk.
    Cuba? Haiti, San Domingo, and Porto Rico.

37 ACCIPITER FRINGILLOIDES Vig.
    West Indian Sharp-shinned Hawk.
    Cuba, Haiti and San Domingo.

38 ACCIPITER GUNDLACHI Lawr.
    Gundlach's Sharp-shinned Hawk.
    Cuba.

39 RUPORNIS RIDGWAYI Cory.
    Ridgway's Hawk.
    San Domingo.

40 PANDION RIDGWAYI Mayn.
    Ridgway's Fish Hawk.
    Bahamas.

41 STRIX FURCATA (Temm).
    Cuban Barn Owl.
    Cuba and Jamaica.

42 STRIX NIGRESCENS Lawr.
    Dusky Barn Owl.
    St. Vincent and Dominica.

43 STRIX GLAUCOPS Kaup.
    Brown Barn Owl.
    Haiti and San Domingo.

44 PSEUDOSCOPS GRAMMICUS (Gosse.)
    Jamaica Owl
    Jamaica.

45 ASIO STYGIUS (Wagl.).
    Cuban Eared Owl.
    Cuba.

46 ASIO PORTORICENSIS Ridgw.
    Porto Rico Eared Owl.
    Porto Rico.

47 GYMNASIO NUDIPES (Daud.).
    West Indian Dwarf Owl.
    Porto Rico, St. John, St. Croix, and St. Thomas.

48 GYMNASIO LAWRENCEII (Scl. & Salv.).
    Lawrence's Owl.
    Cuba.

49 GLAUCIDIUM SIJU (D'Orb.).
    Cuban Pigmy Owl.
    Cuba.

50 SPEOTYTO DOMINICENSIS Cory.
    San Domingo Burrowing Owl.
    Haiti.

51 SPEOTYTO GUADELOUPENSIS (Ridgw.).
    Guadeloupe Burrowing Owl.
    Guadeloupe and St. Nevis.

52 SPEOTYTO AMAURA Lawr.
    Antigua Burrowing Owl.
    Antigua.

53 SPEOTYTO BAHAMENSIS Mayn.
    Bahama Burrowing Owl.
    New Providence, Eleuthera?, Bahamas.

54 ARA TRICOLOR (Bechst.).
    Green Macaw.
    Cuba and Jamaica.

55 CONURUS EUOPS. (Wagl.).
    Cuban Paroquet.
    Cuba.

56 CONURUS XANTHOLAEMUS Scl.
    Orange-cheeked Paroquet.
    St. Thomas and St. Croix.

57 CONURUS NANUS (Vig.).
Jamaica Paroquet.
Jamaica.

58 CONURUS CHLOROPTERUS (Souance.).
San Domingo Paroquet.
SanDomingo.

59 CONURUS GUNDLACHI Caban.
Mona Paroquet.
Mona, near Porto Rico.

60 CHRYSOTIS SALLAEI Scl.
San Domingo Parrot.
Haiti and San Domingo.

61 CHRYSOTIS VITTATA (Bodd.).
Porto Rico Parrot.
Porto Rico.

62 CHRYSOTIS COLLARIA (Linn.).
Blue-headed Parrot.
Jamaica.

63 CHRYSOTIS LEUCOCEPHALA (Linn.).
White-headed Parrot.
Cuba and Bahamas.

64 CHRYSOTIS AGILIS (Linn.).
Jamaica Parrot.
Jamaica.

65 CHRYSOTIS AUGUSTA (Vig.).
Dominica Parrot.
Dominica.

66 CHRYSOTIS GUILDINGI (Vig.).
St. Vincent Parrot.
St. Vincent.

67 CHRYSOTIS CAYMANENSIS Cory.
Cayman Parrot.
Grand Cayman.

68 CHRYSOTIS BOUQUETI (Bechst.).
Purple-throated Parrot.
Dominica.

69 CHRYSOTIS VERSICOLOR (Mull.).
St. Lucia Parrot.
Santa Lucia.

70 SAUROTHERA VETULA (Linn.).
Jamaica Ground Cuckoo.
Jamaica.

71 SAUROTHERA DOMINICENSIS Lafr.
San Domingo Cuckoo.
Haiti and San Domingo.

72 SAUROTHERA VIEILLOTI Bp.
Porto Rico Ground Cuckoo.
Porto Rico.

73 SAUROTHERA MERLINI D'Orb.
Cuban Ground Cuckoo.
Cuba.

74 SAUROTHERA BAHAMENSIS. Bryant.
Bahama Ground Cuckoo.
Bahamas.

75 SAUROTHERA ANDREA Miller.
Andros Ground Cuckoo.
Andros, Bahamas.

76 HYETORNIS PLUVIALIS (Gmel.).
Mountain Cuckoo.
Jamaica.

77 CERYLE STRICTIPENNIS Lawr.
Guadeloupe Kingfisher.
Guadeloupe.

78 TODUS VIRIDIS Linn.
Green Tody.
Jamaica.

79 TODUS ANGUSTIROSTRIS Lafr.
San Domingo Tody.
San Domingo.

80 TODUS SUBULATUS Gould.
Hatian Tody.
Haiti and San Domingo.

81 TODUS PULCHERRIMUS Sharpe.
    Blue-green Tody.
    Jamaica?

82 TODUS HYPOCHONDRIACUS Bryant.
    Porto Rico Tody.
    Porto Rico.

83 TODUS MULTICOLOR Gould.
    Cuban Tody.
    Cuba.

84 PICUMNUS MICROMEGAS Sundev.
    San Domingo Picumnus.
    Haiti and San Domingo.

85 CAMPEPHILUS BAIRDI.
    Baird's Ivory-billed Woodpecker.
    Cuba.

86 DRYOBATES MAYNARDI Ridg.
    Maynard's Woodpecker.
    Northern Bahama Islands.

87 XIPHIDIOPICUS PERCUSSUS (Temm.).
    Cuban Woodpecker.
    Cuba.

88 MELANERPES PORTORICENSIS (Daud.).
    Porto Rico Woodpecker.
    Porto Rico and St. Thomas.

89 MELANERPES L'HERMINIERI (Less.).
    Guadeloupe Woodpecker.
    Guadeloupe.

90 CENTURUS STRIATUS (Mull.).
    Striped Woodpecker.
    Haiti and San Domingo.

91 CENTURUS RADIOLATUS (Wagl.).

    Jamaica Woodpecker.
    Jamaica.

92 CENTURUS SUPERCILIARIS (Temm.).
    Cuban Red-bellied Woodpecker.
    Cuba.

93 CENTURUS CAYMANENSIS Cory.
Cayman Woodpecker.
Grand Cayman.

94 CENTURUS NYEANUS Ridgw.
Wattling Woodpecker.
Wattling's Island, Bahamas.

95 CENTURUS BLAKEI Ridgw.
Abaco Woodpecker.
Abaco, Bahamas.

96 COLAPTES CHRYSOCAULOSUS Gundl.
Cuban Flicker.
Cuba.

97 COLAPTES GUNDLACHI Cory.
Cayman Flicker.
Grand Cayman.

98 NESOCELEUS FERNANDINAE (Vig.).
Cuban Banded Woodpecker.
Cuba.

99 NYCTIBIUS JAMAICENSIS (Gmel.).
Jamaica Night Jar.
Jamaica.

100 NYCTIBIUS PALLIDUS Gosse.
Gosse's Night Jar.
Jamaica.

101 CHORDEILES MINOR Cab.
West Indian Night Hawk.
Antilles.

102 ANTROSTOMUS RUFUS (Bodd.).
Red Goatsucker.
Santa Lucia, West Indies.

103 ANTROSTOMUS CUBANENSIS Lawr.
Cuban Goatsucker.
Cuba.

104 SIPHONORHIS AMERICANUS (Linn.)
Jamaica Goatsucker.
Jamaica.

105 STENOPSIS CAYENNENSIS (Gmel.).
   Cayenne Goatsucker.
   Lesser Antilles?

106 CYPSELUS PHOENIOBIUS (Gosse.).
   White-bellied Swift.
   Cuba, Jamaica, Haiti, and San Domingo.

107 CHAETURA DOMINICANA Lawr.
   Dominica Swift.
   Dominica.

108 HEMIPROCNE ZONARIS (Shaw).
   Collared Swift.
   Jamaica, Cuba and San Domingo.

109 CHAETURA CINEREIVENTRIS Scl.
   Grenada Swift.
   Grenada.

110 CHAETURA BRACHYURA (Jard.).
   Short-tailed Swift.
   St. Vincent and Grenada.

111 GLAUCIS HIRSUTA (Gmel.).
   Grenada Hummer.
   Grenada.

112 LAMPORNIS DOMINICUS (Linn.).
   Green-throated Hummer.
   Haiti, San Domingo, Porto Rico and St. Thomas?

113 LAMPORNIS VIRIDIS (Vieill.).
   Porto Rico Hummer.
   Porto Rico.

114 LAMPORNIS MANGO (Linn.).
   Mango Hummer.
   Jamaica.

115 EULAMPIS JUGULARIS (Linn.).
   Purple-throated Hummer
   Lesser Antilles.

116 EULAMPIS HOLOSERICEUS (Linn.).
   Blue-breasted Hummer.
   Lesser Antilles.

117 AITHURUS POLYTMUS. (Linn.).
Jamaica Long-tailed Hummer.
Jamaica.

118 THALURANIA BICOLOR (Gmel.).
Dominica Hummer.
Dominica.

119 MELLISUGA MINIMA (Linn.).
Vervain Hummer.
Jamaica, Haiti and San Domingo.

120 CALYPTE HELENAE (Gundl.).
Helen's Hummer.
Cuba.

121 DORICHA EVELYNAE (Bourc.).
Bahama Woodstar.
Bahamas.

122 DORICHA LYRURA Gould.
Lyre-tailed Hummer.
Inagua and Long Island.

123 BELLONA CRISTATA (Linn.).
Blue-crested Hummer.
Santa Lucia, Barbadoes, St. Vincent, Martinique and
St. Bartholomew.

124 BELLONA EXILIS (Gmel.).
Green-crested Hummer.
Porto Rico, St. Thomas, Dominica, St. Croix, Mont-
serrat, Nevis, and Martinique.

125 SPORADINUS ELEGANS (Vieill.).
Bronzed Hummer.
Haiti and San Domingo.

126 SPORADINUS RICCORDI (Gerv.).
Riccord's Hummer.
Andros, Bahamas and Cuba.

127 SPORADINUS MAUGAEI (Vieill.).
Blue-tailed Hummer.
Porto Rico.

123 PRIOTELUS TEMNURUS (Temm.).
Cuban Trogan.
Cuba.

129 TEMNOTROGON ROSEIGASTER (Vieill.).
Rose-bellied Trogon.
San Domingo.

130 HADROSTOMUS NIGER (Gmel.).
Dusky Continga.
Jamaica.

131 TYRANNUS MAGNIROSTRIS D'Orb.
Large-billed Kingbird.
Cuba. Inagua?

132 TYRANNUS ROSTRATUS Scl.
Lesser Antillian Kingbird.
Lesser Antilles.

133 BLACICUS MARTINICENSIS Cory. ,
Martinique Flycatcher.
Martinique.

134 BLACICUS FLAVIVENTRIS Lawr.
Grenada Flycatcher.
Grenada.

135 BLACICUS BLANCOI Gundl.
Porto Rico Flycatcher.
Porto Rico.

136 BLACICUS CARIBAEUS (D'Orb.).
Cuban Flycatcher.
Cuba.

137 BLACICUS BARBIROSTRIS (Swains.).
Jamaica Flycatcher.
Jamaica.

138 BLACICUS BRUNNEICAPILLUS Lawr.
Dominica Flycatcher.
Dominica.

139 MYIARCHUS DENIGRATUS Cory.
Cayman Crested Flycatcher.
Grand Gayman.

140 MYIARCHUS BERLEPSCHII Cory.
 St. Kitts Crested Flycatcher.
 St. Kitts.

141 MYIARCHUS DOMINICENSIS (Bryant).
 San Domingo Crested Flycatcher.
 Haiti and San Domingo.

142 MYIARCHUS SCLATERI Lawr.
 Martinique Crested Flycatcher.
 Martinique.

143 MYIARCHUS OBERI Lawr.
 Ober's Crested Flycatcher.
 St. Vincent, Dominica, Santa Lucia, and Grenada.

144 MYIARCHUS ANTILLARUM (Bryant).
 Porto Rico Crested Flycatcher.
 Porto Rico.

145 MYIARCHUS SAGRAE (Gundl.).
 Bahama Crested Flycatcher.
 Cuba and Bahamas.

146 MYIARCHUS STOLIDUS (Gosse).
 Yellow-bellied Crested Flycatcher.
 Jamaica.

147 MYIARCHUS VALIDUS Cab.
 Jamaica Crested Flycatcher.
 Jamaica.

148 CONTOPUS HISPANIOLENSIS (Bryant).
 San Domingo Pewee.
 Haiti and San Domingo.

149 CONTOPUS BAHAMENSIS (Bryant).
 Bahama Pewee.
 Bahamas.

150 CONTOPUS LATIROSTRIS (Verr.).
 St. Lucia Pewee.
 Santa Lucia.

151 CONTOPUS PALLIDUS (Gosse).
 Jamaica Pewee.
 Jamaica.

152 LAWRENCIA NANUS (Lawr.).
Dwarf Flycatcher.
San Domingo.

153 PITANGUS GABBII Lawr.
San Domingo Kingbird.
Haiti and San Domingo.

154 PITANGUS BAHAMENSIS Bryant.
Bahama Kingbird.
New Providence, Bahamas.

155 PITANGUS TAYLORI Scl.
Porto Rico Kingbird.
Porto Rico.

156 PITANGUS CAUDIFASCIATUS (D'Orb.).
Fork-tailed Kingbird.
Cuba and Jamaica.

157 ELAINIA COTTA Gosse.
Jamaica Gray Flycatcher.
Jamaica.

158 ELAINIA FALLAX Scl.
Jamaica Green Flycatcher.
Jamaica.

159 ELAINIA MARTINICA (Linn.).
West Indian Olive Flycatcher.
Lesser Antilles.

160 ELAINIA BARBADENSIS Cory.
Barbadoes Olive Flycatcher.
Barbadoes.

161 ELAINIA PAGANA (Licht.).
Grenada Olive Flycatcher.
Grenada.

162 CORVUS MINUTUS Gundl.
Little Crow.
Cuba.

163 CORVUS NASICUS Temm.
Cuban Crow.
Cuba.

164 CORVUS SOLITARIUS Wurt.
Solitary Crow.
Haiti and San Domingo.

165 CORVUS JAMAICENSIS Gmel.
Jamaica Crow.
Jamaica.

166 CORVUS LEUCOGNAPHALUS Daud.
White-headed Crow.
San Domingo and Porto Rico.

167 QUISCALUS ATROVIOLACEUS D'Orb.
Violaceous Grackle.
Cuba.

168 QUISCALUS GUNDLACHII Cassin.
Gundlach's Grackle.
Cuba.

169 QUISCALUS GUADELOUPENSIS Lawr.
Guadeloupe Grackle.
Guadeloupe.

170 QUISCALUS CRASSIROSTRIS Swains.
Tinkling Grackle.
Jamaica.

171 QUISCALUS LUMINOSUS Lawr.
Grenada Grackle.
Grenada.

172 QUISCALUS BRACHYPTERUS Cassin.
Short-winged Grackle.
Porto Rico.

173 QUISCALUS INFLEXIROSTRIS Swains.
Curved-billed Grackle.
Santa Lucia and Martinique.

174 QUISCALUS FORTIROSTRIS Lawr.
Barbadoes Grackle.
Barbadoes.

175 QUISCALUS CAYMANENSIS Cory.
Cayman Grackle.
Grand Cayman.

176 QUISCALUS NIGER (Bodd.).
Black Grackle.
Haiti and San Domingo.

177 NESOPSAR NIGERRIMUS (Osburn.).
Bluish Grackle.
Jamaica.

178 STURNELLA HIPPOCREPIS Wagl.
Cuban Meadow Lark.
Cuba.

179 AGELAIUS ASSIMILIS Gundl.
Cuban Red-wing.
Cuba.

180 AGELAIUS XANTHOMUS Scl.
Porto Rico Red-wing.
Porto Rico.

181 AEGALIUS BRYANTI Ridgw.
Bahama Red-wing.
Andros and New Providence, Bahamas.

182 AGELAIUS HUMERALIS (Vig.).
Orange-shouldered Blackbird.
Cuba.

183 ICTERUS OBERI Lawr.
- Ober's Oriole.
Montserrat.

184 ICTERUS LEUCOPTERYX (Wagl.).
Jamaica Oriole.
Jamaica.

185 ICTERUS LAUDABILIS Scl.
Santa Lucia Oriole.
Santa Lucia.

189 ICTERUS PORTORICENSIS Bryant.
Porto Rico Oriole.
Porto Rico.

187 ICTERUS DOMINICENSIS (Linn.).
Hatian Oriole.
Haiti and San Domingo.

188 ICTERUS HYPOMELAS (Bonap.).
Cuban Oriole.
Cuba.

189 ICTERUS NORTHROPI Allen.
Northrop's Oriole.
Andros, Bahamas.

190 ICTERUS BONANA (Linn.).
Martinique Oriole.
Martinique.

191 ICTERUS BAIRDI Cory.
Baird's Oriole.
Grand Cayman.

192 SPERMESTES CUCULLATUS (Swains.).
Green-breasted Finch.
Porto Rico.

193 HABROPYGA MELPODA (Vieill.).
Crimson-rumped Finch.
Porto Rico.

194 SICALIS FLAVEOLA (Linn.).
Yellow-bellied Finch.
Jamaica.

195 EUETHEIA ADOXA (Gosse.).
Gray Finch.
Jamaica.

196 EUETHEIA OLIVACEA (Gmel.).
Olive Finch.
Cuba, Jamaica, Haiti, San Domingo and Porto Rico.

197 PYRRHOMITRIS CUCULLATA (Swains.).
Hooded Finch.
Cuba and Porto Rico.

198 LOXIMITRIS DOMINICENSIS (Bryant).
San Domingo Goldfinch.
San Domingo.

199 MELOPYRRHA NIGRA (Linn.).
Cuban Grosbeak.
Cuba.

200 VOLATINIA JACARINA (Linn.).
Black Grosbeak.
Grenada.

201 LOXIGILLA PORTORICENSIS (Daud.)
Porto Rico Grosbeak.
Porto Rico.

202 LOXIGILLA GRANDIS Lawr.
St. Christopher Grosbeak.
St. Christopher.

203 LOXIGILLA ANOXANTHA (Gosse).
Jamaica Grosbeak.
Jamaica.

204 LOXIGILLA NOCTIS (Linn.).
Little Black Grosbeak.
Lesser Antilles.

205 LOXIGILLA NOCTIS SCLATERI Allen.
Santa Lucia Grosbeak.
Santa Lucia.

206 LOXIGILLA VIOLACEA (Linn.).
Bahama Grosbeak.
Bahamas, Jamaica, Haiti, and San Domingo.

207 LOXIGILLA BARBADENSIS Cory.
Barbadoes Grosbeak.
Barbadoes.

208 LOXIGILLA RICHARDSONI Cory.
Richardson's Grosbeak.
St. Lucia.

209 SALTATOR GUADELOUPENSIS Lafr.
Green Tanager.
Guadeloupe and Martinique.

210 CALYPTOPHILUS FRUGIVORUS Cory.
Brown-headed Tanager.
San Domingo.

211 PHOENICOPHILUS POLIOCEPHALUS (Bonap.).
San Domingo Tanager.
San Domingo.

212 PHOENICOPHILUS PALMARUM (Linn.).
Yellow-green Tanager.
Haiti and San Domingo.

213 NESOSPINGUS SPECULIFERUS (Lawr.).
Porto Rico Tanager.
Porto Rico.

214 SPINDALIS NIGRICEPHALA (Jameson).
Jamaica Fruit Finch.
· Jamaica.

215 SPINDALIS PORTORICENSIS (Bryant).
Porto Rico Fruit Finch.
Porto Rico.

216 SPINDALIS MULTICOLOR (Vieill.).
Haitian Fruit Finch.
Haiti and San Domingo.

217 SPINDALIS PRETREI (Less.).
Cuban Fruit Finch.
Cuba.

218 SPINDALIS ZENA (Linn.).
Bahama Fruit Finch.
Bahamas.

219 SPINDALIS ZENA TOWNSENDI Ridgw.
Townsend's Fruit Finch.
Abaco, Bahamas.

220 SPINDALIS SALVINI Cory.
Cayman Fruit Finch.
Grand Cayman.

221 CALLISTE VERSICOLOR Lawr.
Many-colored Fruit Finch.
St. Vincent.

222 CALLISTE CUCULLATA (Swains.).
Grenada Fruit Finch.
Grenada.

223 EUPHONIA SCLATERI Bp.
Porto Rico Euphonia.
Porto Rico.

224 EUPHONIA FLAVIFRONS (Sparrm.)
  Yellow-fronted Euphonia.
  St. Bartholemew, Martinique, Guadeloupe, Domini-
  ca, St. Vincent, Grenada, and St. Lucia.

225 EUPHONIA JAMAICA (Linn.).
  Jamaica Euphonia.
  Jamaica.

226 DULUS NUCHALIS Swains.
  White-naped Chatterer.
  Antilles ?

227 DULUS DOMINICUS (Linn.).
  Haitian Chatterer.
  Haiti and San Domingo.

228 LALETES OSBURNI Scl.
  Osburn's Vireo.
  Jamaica.

229 VIREO CALIDRIS (Linn.).
  West Indian Vireo.
  Jamaica, San Domingo, and Antilles.

230 VIREO GUNDLACHI Lemb.
  Gundlach's Vireo.
  Cuba.

231 VIREO CRASSIROSTRIS (Bryant.).
  Bahama Vireo.
  Bahamas.

232 VIREO CRASSIROSTRIS FLAVESCENS Ridgw.
  Yellow-green Vireo.
  Rum Cay, Conception, Highburn Key, and Little
  Galden Key, Bahamas.

233 VIREO ALLENI Cory.
  Allen's Vireo.
  Cayman Islands.

234 VIREO CAYMANENSIS Cory.
  Grand Cayman Vireo.
  Grand Gayman.

235 VIREO LATIMERI Baird.
  Porto Rico Vireo.
  Porto Rico.

236 VIREO MODESTUS Scl.
Jamaica Vireo.
Jamaica.

237 TACHYCINETA SCLATERI (Cory).
San Domingo Swallow.
San Domingo.

238 TACHYCINETA EUCHRYSEA (Gosse).
Jamaica Swallow.
Jamaica.

239 PROGNE DOMINICENSIS (Gmel.).
West Indian Martin.
San Domingo and Antilles.

240 CHLOROPHANES SPIZA (Linn.).
Black-cheeked Creeper.
Cuba.

241 GLOSSIPTILA RUFICOLLIS (Gmel.).
Jamaica Creeper.
Jamaica.

242 COEREBA CYANEA (Linn.).
Blue-headed Creeper.
Cuba.

243 COEREBA ATRATA (Lawr.).
Black-headed Honey Creeper.
St. Vincent and Grenada.

244 COEREBA MARTINICANA (Reich.).
Green-rumped Honey Creeper.
Santa Lucia and Martinique.

245 COEREBA BARBADENSIS (Baird).
Barbadoes Honey Creeper.
Barbadoes.

246 COEREBA DOMINICANA (Taylor).
Dusky Honey Creeper.
Dominica, Antigua, Barbuda, Nevis, St. Eustatius, Guadeloupe, and Saba.

247 COEREBA NEWTONI (Baird.)
St. Croix Honey Creeper.
St. Croix.

248 COEREBA FLAVEOLA (Linn.).
Jamaica Honey Creeper.
Jamaica.

249 COEREBA SACCHARINA (Lawr.).
Grenada Honey Creeper.
St. Vincent and Grenada.

250 COEREBA BARTHOLEMICA (Sparrm.).
St. Bartholemew Honey Creeper.
St. Bartholemew.

251 COEREBA BANANIVORA (Gmel.).
San Domingo Honey Creeper.
San Domingo.

252 COEREBA SANCTI-THOMAE (Ridgw.).
St. Thomas Honey Creeper.
St. Thomas and St. John.

253 COEREBA PORTORICENSIS (Bryant).
Porto Rico Honey Creeper.
Porto Rico and St. Thomas.

254 COEREBA SHARPEI Cory.
Cayman Honey Creeper.
Cayman Islands.

255 TERETISTRIS FORNSI Gundl.
Gray-backed Warbler.
Eastern part of Cuba.

256 TERETISTRIS FERNANDINAE (Lemb.).
Gray-bellied Warbler.
Western part of Cuba.

257 MICROLIGEA PALUSTRIS Cory.
San Domingo Swamp Warbler.
San Domingo.

258 GEOTHLYPIS ROSTRATA Bryant.
Greater Bahama Yellow Throat.
New Providence, Bahamas.

259 GEOTHLYPIS CORYI Ridgw.
Cory's Yellow Throat.
Eleuthera, Bahamas.

260 **GEOTHLYPIS TANNERI** Ridgw.
Tanner's Yellow Throat.
Abaco, Bahamas.

261 **GEOTHLYPIS RESTRICTA** Mayn.
Lesser Bahama Yellow Throat.
New Providence, Bahamas.

262 **CATHAROPEZA BISHOPI** (Lawr.).
St. Vincent Warbler.
St. Vincent.

263 **LEUCOPEZA SEMPERI** Scl.
Santa Lucia Warbler.
Santa Lucia.

264 **DENDROICA PLUMBEA** Lawr.
· Plumbeous Warbler.
Guadeloupe and Dominica.

265 **DENDROICA VITELLINA**
Cayman Warbler. Cory.
Grand Cayman.

266 **DENDROICA AUROCAPILLA** Ridgw.
Golden-headed Warbler.
Grand Cayman and Cayman Brac.

267 **DENDROICA PITYOPHILA** (Gundl.).
Cuban Warbler.
Cuba.

268 **DENDROICA BAHAMENSIS** Mayn.
Bahama Pine Warbler.
New Providence, Bahamas.

269 **DENDROICA ADELAIDAE** Baird.
Adelaide's Warbler.
Porto Rico.

270 **DENDROICA DELICATA** Ridgw.
Santa Lucia Warbler.
Santa Lucia.

271 **DENDROICA PHARETRA** (Gosse).
Arrow-head Warbler.
Jamaica.

272 DENDROICA EOA (Gosse).
Jamaica Warbler.
Jamaica.

273 DENDROICA RUFIGULA Baird.
Martinique Warbler.
Martinique.

274 DENDROICA CAPITALIS Lawr.
Barbadoes Warbler.
Barbadoes.

275 DENDROICA RUFICAPILLA (Gmel.).
Rufous-crowned Warbler.
Barbuda, Antigua, Porto Rico, and St. Thomas.

276 DENDROICA MELANOPTERA Lawr.
Black-winged Warbler.
Guadeloupe and Dominica.

277 DENDROICA GUNDLACHI Baird.
Gundlach's Warbler.
Cuba. Andros and New Providence, Bahamas.

278 DENDROICA PETECHIA (Linn.).
Jamaica Warbler.
Jamaica.

279 THRYOTHORUS GRENADENSIS Lawr.
Grenada Wren.
Grenada.

280 THRYOTHORUS MUSICUS Lawr.
St. Vincent Wren.
St. Vincent.

281 THRYOTHORUS RUFESCENS Lawr.
Rufous Wren.
Dominica and Guadeloupe.

282 THRYOTHORUS MARTINICENSIS Scl.
Martinique Wren.
Martinique.

283 THRYOTHORUS GUADELOUPENSIS Cory.
Guadeloupe Wren.
Grand Terre, Guadeloupe.

284 THRYOTHORUS MESOLEUCUS Scl.
Santa Lucia Wren.
Santa Lucia.

285 POLIOPTILA LEMBEYI (Gundl.).
Cuban Gnatcatcher.
Cuba.

286 POLIOPTILA CAESIOGASTER Ridgw.
Bahama Blue-gray Gnatcatcher.
Bahamas.

287 MYIADESTES ARMILLATUS (Vieill.).
Vieillotte's Solitaire.
Martinique.

288 MYIADESTES ELIZABETH (Lemb.).
Cuban Solitaire.
Cuba.

289 MYIADESTES SOLITARIUS Baird.
Jamaica Solitaire.
Jamaica.

290 MYIADESTES MONTANUS Cory.
Haitian Solitaire.
Haiti.

291 MYIADESTES DOMINICANUS Stejn.
Dominica Solitaire.
Dominica.

292 MYIADESTES SANCTAE-LUCIAE Stejn.
Santa Lucia Solitaire.
Santa Lucia.

293 MYIADESTES GENIBARBIS Swains.
Martinique Solitaire.
Martinique.

294 MYIADESTES SIBILANS Lawr.
St. Vincent Solitaire.
St. Vincent.

295 MIMUS HILLII March.
Hill's Mocking Bird.
Jamaica

296 MIMUS GUNDLACHI Caban.
  Cuban Mocking Bird.
  Cuba.

297 MIMUS BAHAMENSIS Bryant.
  Bahama Mocking Bird.
  Northern Bahamas.

298 MIMUS GILVUS (Vieill.)
  Lesser Antillian Mocking Bird.
  St. Vincent, Grenada, Santa Lucia, and St. Thomas.

299 MIMUS DOMINICUS (Linn.).
  San Domingo Mocking Bird.
  Haiti and San Domingo.

300 MIMUS ELEGANS Sharpe.
  Inagua Mocking Bird.
  Inagua and Eleuthera, Bahamas.

301 MIMUS ORPHEUS (Linn.).
  Jamaica Mocking Bird.
  Jamaica and Grand Cayman.

302 CINCLOCERTHIA GUTTURALIS (Lafr.).
  Martinique Thrush.
  Martinique.

303 CINCLOCERTHIA MACRORHYNCHA Scl.
  Santa Lucia Thrush.
  Santa Lucia.

304 CINCLOCERTHIA RUFICAUDA (Gould).
  Red-tailed Thrush.
  Guadeloupe and Dominica.

305 RAMPHOCINCLUS BRACHYURUS (Vieill.).
  Martinique Curved-billed Thrush.
  Martinique.

806 RAMPHOCINCLUS SANCTAE-LUCIAE. Cory.
  Santa Lucia Curved-billed Thrush.
  St. Lucia.

307 MARGAROPS MONTANUS (Lafr.).
  Mountain Fruit Thrush.
  Martinique, St. Vincent, Dominica, Santa Lucia,
Guadeloupe and Grenada.

31

308 MARGAROPS MONTANUS ALBIVENTRIS (Lawr.)
    Lawrence's Fruit Thrush.
    Grenada.

309 MARGAROPS MONTANUS RUFUS Cory.
    Cory's Fruit Thrush.
    Santa Lucia.

310 MARGAROPS DENSIROSTRIS (Vieill.).
    White-throated Fruit Thrush.
    Dominica, Martinique, Monsterrat, Santa Lucia and
    Guadeloupe.

311 MARGAROPS FUSCATUS (Vieill.).
    Paw-paw Fruit Thrush.
    Inagua, Bahamas; Porto Rico, San Domingo? St.
Thomas and St. Croix.

312 CICHLHERMINIA DOMINICENSIS (Lawr.).
    Yellow-legged Thrush.
    Dominica.

313 CICHLHERMINIA SANCTAE-LUCIAE (Scl.).
    Santa Lucia Thrush.
    Santa Lucia.

314 CICHLHERMINIA HERMINIERI (Lafr.).
    Guadeloupe Thrush.
    Guadeloupe and Martinique.

315 MIMOCICHLA ARDESIACA (Vieill.).
    San Domingo Thrush.
    San Domingo.

316 MIMOCICHLA PLUMBEA (Linn.).
    Plumbeous Thrush.
    New Providence, Andros and Abaco, Bahamas.

317 MIMOCICHLA SCHISTACEA Baird.
    Cuban Thrush.
    Eastern part of Cuba.

318 MIMOCICHLA RUBRIPES (Temm.).
    Red-legged Thrush.
    Cuba.

319 MIMOCICHLA RAVIDA Cory.
    Cayman Thrush.
    Grand Cayman and Cayman Brac.

32

320 **MERULA NIGRIROSTRIS** (Lawr.).
Black-billed Thrush.
St. Vincent.

321 **MERULA GYMNOPHTHALMA** (Caban.).
Pale Thrush.
Grenada. Trinidad and Tobago.

322 **MERULA AURANTIA** (Gmel.).
White-winged Thrush.
Jamaica.

323 **MERULA JAMAICENSIS** (Gmel.).
Jamaica Thrush.
Jamaica.

APPENDIX TO CATALOGUE

OF THE BIRDS OF THE WEST INDIES.

BY

C. J. MAYNARD.

DESCRIPTION OF NEW SPECIES.

As the publication of the conclusion of Vol. III of my Contributions to Science has been greatly delayed, and as I wish to distribute this catalogue, so long withheld, I have given a brief description of the new species mentioned, referring the reader to the volume of Contributions, mentioned in the introduction, for further descriptions and figures.

15 COLINUS BAHAMENSIS
Bahama Bob-white

Size, form, and general coloration, of the Florida Bobwhite, Colinus v. floridanus, but differs in having narrower black bandings below which show a tendency to form arrow shaped markings· The chestnut is also richer. Habitat, the island of New Providence. Types male and female in my collection.

53 SPEOTYTO BAHAMENSIS.
Bahama Burrowing Owl.

Intermediate, in coloration between S. floridana and S. dominicensis, thus differing from both. Habitat, New Providence and probably Eleuthera.. Type, a female in my collection.

268 DENDROICA BAHAMENSIS
Bahama Pine Warbler

Similar to Dendroica vigorsii, but paler in general coration, especially below where the color is decidedly yellow, not greenish yellow. Habitat, New Providence. Types, male and female in my collection.

Species described provisionally and not given in the list.

HAEMOTOPUS PRATTII
Pratt's Oyster Catcher.

Similar to the H. palliatus, but differs in having a stouter, thicker bill, and in being much lighter in color above, but with the dark of the back encroaching upon the white of the rump. Types in my collection taken on Flemming's Key, Bahamas, April 29, 1893, but probably occurs throughout the islands as a resident.

I have named this species for my friend, Marland L. Pratt to whom this catalogue is dedicated.

Actual date of issue, November twenty-ninth, 1899.

29 COLUMBIGALLINA JAMAICENSIS.
Jamaica Ground Dove.

Similar to C. bahamensis, but differs in being lighter in shade and in having the bill distinctly yellow at the base. Types, male and female, in the Bryant Collection.

This is not the C. passerina of Linnaeus : he, having no type, based his description mainly upon Catesby's figure of the Ground Dove of the Carolinas. This figure, although good, is sparrow-like enough in form to have evidently suggested the name of passerina to Linnaeus.

APPENDIX TO CATALOGUE

OF THE BIRDS OF THE WEST INDIES.
BY
C. J. MAYNARD.

DESCRIPTION OF NEW SPECIES.

As the publication of the conclusion of Vol. III of my Contributions to Science has been greatly delayed, and as I wish to distribute this catalogue, so long withheld, I have given a brief description of the new species mentioned, referring the reader to the volume of Contributions, mentioned in the Introduction, for further descriptions and figures.

15 COLINUS BAHAMENSIS.
Bahama Bob-white.

Size, form, and general coloration of the Florida Bob-white, *Colinus v. floridans*, but differs in having narrower black bandings below which show a tendency to form arrow-shaped markings. The chestnut is also richer. Habitat, the Island of New Providence. Types, male and female in my collection.

53 SPEOTYTO BAHAMENSIS.
Bahama Burrowing Owl.

Intermediate between *S. floridanus* and *S. dominicencis*, thus differing from both. Habitat, New Providence, and probably Eleuthera. Type, a female in my collection.

267 DENDROICA BAHAMENSIS.
Bahama Pine Warbler.

Similar to *Dendroica vigorsii*, but paler in general coloration, especially below, where the color is decidedly yellow, not greenish-yellow. Habitat, New Providence. Type, male and female in my collection.

Species described provisionally and not given in the list.

13.1 HAEMATOPUS PRATTII.
Pratt's Oyster Catcher.

Similar to *H. palliatus*, but differs in having a stouter, thicker bill, and in being much lighter in color above, but with the dark of the back encroaching upon the white of the rump.   Types in my collection taken on Flemming's Key, Bahamas, April 29, 1897, but probably occurs throughout the islands as a resident.

I have named this species for my friend, Marland L. Pratt, to whom this catalogue is dedicated.

Actual date of issue, November twenty-ninth, 1899.

29 COLUMBIGALLINA JAMAICENSIS.
Jamaica Ground Dove.

Similar to *C. bahamensis*, but differs in being lighter in shade and in having the bill distinctly yellow at the base.   Types, male and female, in the Bryant Collection.

This is not the *C. passerina* of Linnaeus; he, having no type, based his description mainly upon Catesby's figure of the Ground Dove of the Carolinas.   This figure, although good, is Sparrow-like enough in form to have evidently suggested the name of *passerina* to Linnaeus.

35

SECOND APPENDIX.
ADDITIONS AND CORRECTIONS.

In November, 1899, a small edition of the first Appendix to this catalogue was issued, but the catalogue itself was withheld. It is now published with the first appendix printed as it then appeared. Through an inadvertence I quite overlooked Mr. Cory's Review of the Birds of the West Indies printed in the Auk for October, 1891, thus in two cases I have used names in describing birds that he had used for different species of the same genera (see Nos. 53 and 268). Corrections, in the catalogue and additions, changes etc. in it, appear in the following pages, approximately bringing the catalogue up to date. I have not, however, for several reasons, always given all of the generic changes that Mr. Ridgway has given in his Birds of North and Middle America, or that have been recently published by other authors.

Believing, as I do, that sub-specific names should be given only to birds which intergrade with allied forms through intermingling at points of actual contact, I cannot consider insular forms as sub-specific, for they are barred by isolation from this intergradation.

Types of the species described mentioned as being in my collection are now in the Bangs Collection.

17.1 ORTALIS RUFICAUDATA Jard.
Red-tailed Chachalaca.
Union Island and Grenada.

29.1 COLUMBIGALLINA AFLAVIDA Palmer & Riley.
Cuban Ground Dove.
Cuba.

25 For Grenada Ground Dove, read Grenada Dove.

25.1 ZENAIDA CASTANEA (Wagl).
Antillian Dove.
Most of the Lesser Antilles.

25.2 ZENAIDA VINACEORUFA Ridgw.
Ridgway's Dove.
Grenada and Grenadines.

36

29.2 ZENAIDURA BELLA Palmer & Riley.
Cuban Mourning Dove.
Cuba.

31.1 GEOTRYGON SABAE Riley.
Saba Quail Dove.
Saba Island.

39.1 RUPORNIS MAGNIROSTRIS Kaup.
Martinique Hawk.
Martinique.

53 Change to, **SPEOTYTO CAVICOLA** Bangs.
Bahama Burrowing Owl.
New Providence.

56 Erase St. Croix.

59 According to Cory, C. gundlaci Cabn. proves to be
C. chloropterus (Souance).

76.1 COCCYZUS DOMINICAE Shelly.
Large-billed Cuckoo.
St. Lucia, Grenada, Dominica, and Porto Rico.

95.1 CENTURUS BAHAMENSIS Cory.
Great Bahama Woodpecker.
Great Bahama.

101.1 CHORDEILES VICINUS Riley.
Bahaman Nighthawk.
Bahama Islands.

108 For **HEMIPROCNE**, read **CHAETURA**.

114.1 LAMPORNIS VIRGINALIS Gould.
Porto Rico Hummer.
Porto Rico.

117.1 AITHURUS SCITULUS Brewster & Bangs.
Graceful Long-tailed Hummer.
North-eastern Jamaica.

124.1 BELLONA ORNATUS Gould.
St. Vincent Hummer.
St. Vincent.

37

126.1 SPORADINUS AENEOVIRIDIS (Palmer & Riley).
Abaco Hummer.
Abaco.

132.1 TYRANNUS CUBENSIS Richm.
Cuban Kingbird.
Cuba.

148 to 151, inclusive, should be referred to the genus
BLACICUS.

155.1 PITANGUS JAMAICENSIS Chapm.
Jamaica Kingbird.
Jamaica.

161.1 ELANIA CHERRIEI Cory.
San Domingo Flycatcher.
San Domingo.

173. Erase, and Martinque.

173.1 HOLOQUISCALUS MARTINICENSIS Ridgw.
Martinique Grackle.
Martinique.

[Note: All of the West Indian Grackles should be referred
to the genus **HOLOQUISCALUS**, excepting No. 167 which is
a **PTILOXENA**, and No. 177 which remains as it is.

192.1 COTURNICULUS SAVANNARUM (Gmel).
Antillian Grasshopper Sparrow.
Jamaica and Porto Rico.

196.1 EUETHEIA CORYI Ridgw.
Cory's Grassquit.
Cayman Brac.

196.2 EUETHEIA BRYANTI Ridgw.
Bryant's Grassquit.
Porto Rico.

196.3 EUETHEIA OMISSA Jard.
Carib Grassquit.
Cuba, Porto Rico, and the Lesser Antilles.

38

196.4 EUETHEIA MARCHII (Baird.)
March's Grassquit.
Jamaica, Hayti, Barbados and Grenada

196.5 MELANOSPIZA RICHARDSONI Cory.
Richardson's Grassquit.
St. Lucia.

197.1 SPOROPHILA GUTTURALIS (Licht.)
Yellow-bellied Seedeater.
Grenada.

198.1 MELOPYRRHA TAYLORI Hartert.
Grand Cayman Bullfinch.
Grand Cayman.

204.1 PYRRHULAGRA DOMINICANA Ridgw.
Dominican Grosbeak.
Dominica, Grand Terre, Marie Galante, Desirado, and Grenada.

[Note: **PYRRHULARGA** has priority over **LOXIGILLA**.]

204.2 PYRRHULAGRA CRISSALIS Ridgw.
St. Vincent Grosbeak.
St. Vincent.

204.3 PYRRHULAGRA RIDGEWAYI Cory.
Antigua Grosbeak.
Antigua.

204.4 PYRRHULAGRA CORYI Ridgw.
Cory's Grosbeak.
St, Eustatius and St. Christopher.

204.5 PYRRHULAGRA GRENADENSIS Cory.
Grenada Grosbeak.
Grenada.

206.1 PYRRHULAGRA RUFICOLLIS (Gmelin).
Jamaican Grosbeak.
Jamaica.

206.2 PYRRHULAGRA AFFINIS Baird.
Haitian Grosbeak.
Haiti.

39

243. COEREBA WELLSI Cory.
Wells' Honey Creeper.
Granada.

259.1 GEOTHLYPIS MAYNARDI Bangs.
Maynard's Yellow-throat.
New Providence.

260.2 GEOTHLYPIS INCOMPTA Ridgw.
Lesser Abaco Yellow-throat.
Abaco.

260.3 GEOTHLYPIS EXIGUA Ridgw.
Andros Yellow-throat.
Andros Island.

260.4 GEOTHLYPIS FLAVIDA Ridgw.
Luteous Yellow-throat.
New Providence.

267.1 DENDROICA BAHAMENSIS Cory.
Bahama Warbler.
Abaco and Great Bahama.

268 Change to **DENDROICA ACHRUSTERA** Bangs.
New Providence Pine Warbler.
New Providence.

268.1 DENDROICA ABACOENSIS Ridgw.
Abaco Pine Warbler.
Abaco.

273 to 278, inclusive, should be referred to the genus CHRYSOCANTOR Mayn. (see Warblers of New England, p. 58), to which add;

278.1 CHRYSOCANTOR FLAVICEPS Chapm.
Bahama Yellow Warbler.
Andros, New Providence, and Inagua.

301.1 MIMUS PORTORICENSIS Bryant.
Porto Rico Mockingbird
Porto Rico.

40

312.1 CICHLHERMINIA LAWRENCII Cory.
Lawrence's Thrush.
Montserrat.

315.1 MIMOCICHLA ALBIVENTRIS Sclater.
White-vented Thrush.
San Domingo.

A few species of accidental or of uncertain occurrence, and a few others the specific status of each of which is unsettled, are omitted from the foregoing list. A few recently added species may have been overlooked.

The date of the issue of the complete catalogue is December 1, 1903.

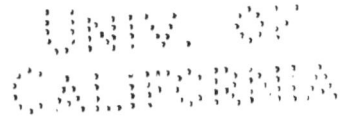
UNIV. OF
CALIFORNIA

www.ingramcontent.com/pod-product-compliance
Lightning Source LLC
Chambersburg PA
CBHW030004030726
47499CB00008B/2882